Scottish, Welsh & Irish Inspirations

Edited by Michelle Afford

Young Writers
First published in Great Britain in 2007 by:
Young Writers
Remus House
Coltsfoot Drive
Peterborough
PE2 9JX
Telephone: 01733 890066
Website: www.youngwriters.co.uk

SB ISBN 978-1 84602 851 9

Foreword

Young Writers was established in 1991 and has been passionately devoted to the promotion of reading and writing in children and young adults ever since. The quest continues today. Young Writers remains as committed to the nurturing of poetic and literary talent as ever.

This year's Young Writers competition has proven as vibrant and dynamic as ever and we are delighted to present a showcase of the best poetry from across the UK and in some cases overseas. Each poem has been selected from a wealth of *A Pocketful Of Rhyme* entries before ultimately being published in this, our fourteenth primary school poetry series.

Once again, we have been supremely impressed by the overall quality of the entries we have received. The imagination, energy and creativity which has gone into each young writer's entry made choosing the poems a challenging and often difficult but ultimately hugely rewarding task - the general high standard of the work submitted ensured this opportunity to bring their poetry to a larger appreciative audience.

We sincerely hope you are pleased with this final collection and that you will enjoy *A Pocketful Of Rhyme Scottish, Welsh & Irish Inspirations* for many years to come.

Contents

The Poems

The Volcano

The volcano is a furious king of heat,
It dribbles out its anger to demolish everything in its path.
It crashes and crackles, explodes at any time
And will put you in a lava bath.

A volcano is a beast, a lord of burn,
It fills people with hate and sorrow.
It preys on villages and people you know
And will get you sometime tomorrow.

Joseph Jennings-Harrison (9)

Yellow

Yellow is bright
Yellow is the sun
Yellow is the colour
When you are having fun
Yellow is amazing
Yellow is cool
Yellow reminds me
Of sitting in a pool
Yellow is the sun
Up in the sky
Yellow is a colour
That will not lie
Yellow is speedy
Yellow is fast
Yellow is the colour
That I think of in class
Yellow is nice
Yellow is fair
Yellow is the colour
Of my lovely blonde hair.

Anna Tennyson (9)
Ballyoran Controlled Primary School, Portadown

Ladybird

Ladybird, oh ladybird
Why are you red with black dots?
Are you always like this?
I am confused or is it you?

Ladybird, oh ladybird
You're so nice in the air
When you fly so high
When you land, we try to catch you
You're too beautiful and we love you.

Ladybird, oh ladybird
Is your red a sign of danger?
People say you only live for one day
But how can this be
When you are so beautiful?

Laura Breen (8)
Ballyoran Controlled Primary School, Portadown

My Dog

My dog I called Ellie
She is always biting me
I like her and she likes me
Together we're a family
I always hide from her
She always hides from me.
I love her and she loves me
Together we're a family
We can play all day
I play with her, she plays with me
Together we're a family.

Mary-Anna Creaney (8)
Ballyoran Controlled Primary School, Portadown

Dragons

A puff of dragon smoke,
Swirling in the night sky.
Those yellow strong
Razor-blade teeth.
That long green
Spiky, sharp tail.

Those evil red eyes,
Light up in the dark sky.
The loud noise when
They stamp their feet.
The deafening noise
When they growl.

When they fight
The destruction they make.
Their tails swing
And hit the walls.
Their sharp claws
Kill their enemies.

Matthew McBride (10)
Ballyoran Controlled Primary School, Portadown

Anacondas

Anacondas sneak,
Anacondas hunt,
Anacondas slither,
Anacondas kill.
If you're ever in the Amazon please
Beware!
If an anaconda sees you
You'll make a great meal
So there!

Ross Heaney (10)
Ballyoran Controlled Primary School, Portadown

Flowers

Flowers are a beautiful creation of life.
When you see the first snowdrop
The coldness leaves you.
The warmth you feel with the heat of the sun
Is like being wrapped in cotton wool.
Suddenly the winter's gone
And the daffodil arrives too.
Spring is here, it's time to smile,
Next we know the rose is here,
The true holiday time has come.
But all too soon the sun cools down
And the leaves on the trees fall,
Becoming crisp and brown.
It won't be long before it's cold
And you want to see the rose again.

Siridean Larkin (9)
Ballyoran Controlled Primary School, Portadown

Things I Like Doing

Spending time with my godparents
At their house.
Eating toast
And drinking hot tea.
Colouring with my niece,
Going to Jumping Jacks
With my family.
Walking my dog Ellie
Around the shops,
With my godparents.
These are the things I like.

Darren Creaney (9)
Ballyoran Controlled Primary School, Portadown

What Are Aeroplanes?

They are cheetahs in the sky,
They are giant birds that don't move their wings,
They are eagles ready to kill,
They are meteors without a trail,
They are falcons in the sky,
They are giant missiles shooting like a star,
They are fireworks without explosions,
I think they are helpless little birds flying from death,
They are bullets shooting from battleships,
They are rockets shooting from the ground,
They are humans with wings,
They are human missiles,
They are rockets on a mission with a caution of death.

Adam McCaffrey (11)
Ballyoran Controlled Primary School, Portadown

To Dad

I wish the old days would come back
With all the fun and all the craic
The games and football with my friends
I'm sad it all had to end

I miss the way we used to laugh
Your silly jokes were always daft
I can't believe I'll never see
Your big brown eyes look back at me

I know that Heaven is your home
So just for you I wrote this poem
And even though Dad we're apart
You'll live forever in my heart.

Nualagh Coleman (8)
Ballyoran Controlled Primary School, Portadown

Butterfly

Butterfly, oh butterfly
Where do you come from?
Where do you go?
In through the back door
And out my window.

Butterfly, oh butterfly
Who do you play with?
Where are your friends?
Chasing the pretty wildflowers
By the winding river bends.

Butterfly, oh butterfly
Were you born with those patterns?
Did someone paint you?
God must be a great artist,
I'd love to be like you.

Amy Breen (8)
Ballyoran Controlled Primary School, Portadown

Jumping Frogs

The jumping frogs are in town,
They're splashing in the lake,
They're driving everyone mad,
Day or night it's just the same.

The people can't catch the frogs,
They're under the water,
They're in the garden,
They're in the house,
They're driving everyone mad,
Day or night it's just the same.

Barry Spence (7)
Ballyoran Controlled Primary School, Portadown

The Qualifiers

Motorbikes, motorbikes, motorbikes,
KTM, Suzuki and Yamaha
Are all good bikes,
Who will be the qualifiers today
Between these three teams?
KTM has stopped for a change of driver,
OK, here we are number 2.
In first place, he's going well,
Oh no number 4 for the Yamaha team has fallen,
This is a disaster.

He has broken his arm,
He is badly hurt
And the bike is in bits,
The throttle is stuck
And the bike will not stop.
OK, the driver has turned it off.
And that's it, it's the end of the race.
It's a good day for the Suzuki team,
They have qualified for the championship,
It's all over and the KTM team have qualified too,
That's it until next week.

John Hatton (11)
Ballyoran Controlled Primary School, Portadown

I Love Horses

Horses are cute
They run and jump
They eat all day and play in the hay
I love riding my horse
When he gallops in the field.

My uncle owns three beautiful horses
Two white and one brown
He is my favourite
I go out on them every weekend
When I go to my uncle's house.

Rachel Mossey (10)
Ballyoran Controlled Primary School, Portadown

Things I Like

Stroking my dog,
He is very fluffy,
Going for walks
In the dark,
Lying in on
Weekend mornings,
Kicking a football
Against the wall,
Drinking tea on a
Cold winter's night,
Going swimming on
Friday afternoons,
But most of all,
Spending time with
My family.

Catherine Cusack (10)
Ballyoran Controlled Primary School, Portadown

Winter

Winter is here
Where is Santa?
I've built a snowman
Where is Santa?
I can't wait for him to come
Where is Santa?
I hope I'll get my presents,
Where is Santa?
It's cold outside,
But I know Santa will come.

Aurimas Andrijaitis (8)
Ballyoran Controlled Primary School, Portadown

Purple

Purple is royal
And very loyal
It can be bright
And just like a light
Purple is a grape
Or a queen's cape
It's the lovely night-time sky
Or can be purple dye
A purple marker
A purple crayon
A purple pastel
A purple spray-on
You feel purple when you're tired
It's the colour I've always admired.

Aiden McNally (9)
Ballyoran Controlled Primary School, Portadown

Puppies

I think puppies
Are rather nice.
Their tails are fluffy,
Their faces cute,
Their ears are pink,
Their teeth are white,
They sleep so cute at night,
They scratch things they shouldn't scratch,
They creep in doors without a latch.

But I think
Puppies are
Really, really nice.

Charlotte Conway (9)
Ballyoran Controlled Primary School, Portadown

All My Dogs

I've got eleven dogs at home
And every one of them my own
Some are big and some are small
It's very hard to feed them all.

Some eat more and some eat less
Which one is my favourite? Guess
I love each one of them the same
And gave each one a special name.

I'd love to take my dogs to school
And to the shops and swimming pool
My friends all think I've lost my head
I think I'll keep them home instead.

Chloe Metcalfe (9)
Ballyoran Controlled Primary School, Portadown

What Happens At Night?

Do the trees come alive
And pick each other's leaves?
Do they?
Who knows? (Not I.) Do you?

Do the stars play tig
In the deep dark blue sky?
Do they?
Who knows? (Not I.) Do you?

Do you now what happens at night?

Erin Conway (11)
Ballyoran Controlled Primary School, Portadown

Planes

When you look up in the sky,
You might see a weird thing flying up high.
From where you stand it looks quite small,
But really they're not small at all.

They're called planes, those things in the sky,
You know, those things flying up high.
The food in the plane isn't that great,
In fact their food is what I hate.

One thing that I like is that they have a TV
And each day they show a different DVD.
If you're going very far it could be over a day,
So remember to bring something for you to play.

Luke Dowd (10)
Ballyoran Controlled Primary School, Portadown

The Bracken Bro

In school one day
My frog teacher said,
'We are going to the Bracken Bro,
Where the fairies grow.'

It's never night,
It stays light,
Puppies sing and run about.

Nothing can hurt you,
Nothing can sting,
It's an everlasting life,
For you and the Bracken Bro king.

Aoife Tennyson (10)
Ballyoran Controlled Primary School, Portadown

My Best Friend Cara

My friend is Cara,
She is pretty and clever.
Cara likes cake,
She is my best friend.
We never fight,
We like to have sleepovers.
I go to Cara's house every Monday and Saturday,
Cara comes to my house every Friday and Sunday.

Morgan Eadie (7)
Ballyoran Controlled Primary School, Portadown

Dinosaurs

If a brontosaurus ever stood before us,
He would simply explore us,
But then ignore us,
In the stomach of a brontosaurus leaves came before us.

If a tyrannosaurus ever saw us,
He would simply adore us,
For the stomach of a tyrannosaurus
Is where he would like to store us.

Rebecca McGuigan (10)
Ballyoran Controlled Primary School, Portadown

Puppies

I love puppies
Because they're cuddly.
They're nice and soft
And really cute.
They would lick you
And fetch a stick for you.
And that's all I've got to say,
Now I'm off to go and play.

Conor Robinson (9)
Ballyoran Controlled Primary School, Portadown

The Puppy!

When I come home from school each day
I run to my puppy
I feed her every day

I walk her around the green

I call her Molly
She is so good and jolly

I love my puppy so much
I'll never let her go.

Caithlin Hackett (10)
Ballyoran Controlled Primary School, Portadown

Birds

I think birds can fly so high
High up into the wonderful sky
Oh, the birds they sway, sway, sway
They sing and flap the day away
They sing so sweetly
It melts into my heart
I just love them so, so much
I never want to part.

Saraid Donnelly (11)
Ballyoran Controlled Primary School, Portadown

I Like Chimpanzees

Chimpanzees swing,
They sleep
And groom each other.
They take people's stuff,
They howl a lot
And if that's not enough,
They're as smart as us!

Keith McAlinden (10)
Ballyoran Controlled Primary School, Portadown

People And Animals

A baby eats
Adults like sweets.

People like swimming
Ducks like to waddle.

An animal moves all kinds of ways
And people run and jump all day.

Animals scratch
So do we.

They run fast
Faster than me.

They would catch
Their prey

And we would sit there
Crying all day.

They wouldn't cry if
Their owner died.

They might stay
By their owner's side.

Connie McCrory (10)
Ballyoran Controlled Primary School, Portadown

The Footballer

There he went, running with pride,
The other team couldn't catch him but they tried.
He put it in the back of the net,
Finally someone got him and he went down in agony.

The manager said, 'No more goals for you!'
There was a corner so he limped on and he shouted,
'Wait, wait!'
He put it in the back of the net,
'There's nothing wrong with my head at least,' he said.

Paul McGinnell (11)
Ballyoran Controlled Primary School, Portadown

That's My Daddy

Couch snoozer
Big boozer
Football mad
Crazy lad
Funny farter
Car starter
Fast driver
Stay aliver
Big tickles man
Loves Snickers man
King of the sofa
Rocking roller
Big joker
Likes 'Max and Paddy'
He's my daddy
I love my daddy.

Megan Sambrook (9)
Bryn Deva CP School, Connahs Quay

My Fantasy

. . . Where skies are blue
Where no one judges you
The trees are green
A beautiful scene.

But when I open my eyes
I see grey skies
The trees are brown
An awful town.

In my fantasy no one cares
In real life everyone's scared.

Disease, contamination and crime
That's what it's like in modern times.

Oh, how I would love to be in my fantasy!

Lauren Andrews (10)
Durand Primary School, Caldicot

A Teacher

Loving teacher
Marking hater
PE lover
Maths hater
Strict teacher
Messy worker
Child lover
Fast runner
Netball lover
Writing lover.
Who am I?

Ryan Worlock (10)
Durand Primary School, Caldicot

The Panda!

Leaf eater
Bamboo keeper
Big feeter
Heavy sleeper
Black-eyed freaker
Sometimes cheater
Enough about a panda
Oh but one more thing
Her name is Amanda.

Racheal Kiely (10)
Durand Primary School, Caldicot

The Man With A Beard

There was a man with a beard
Who said, 'It is just as I feared
Two owls and a bear
Four larks and a wren
Have all built their nests in my beard.'

Jason Lewis (9)
Durand Primary School, Caldicot

Guess Who?

Water drinker
Leaf eater
Brown and yellow
Hates capture
Wild liker
Standing sleeper
Strange galloper
Tall neck
What am I?

Laura Hennesey (9)
Durand Primary School, Caldicot

Guess Who?

Dark grey
Heavy stomper
Lumpy walker
Dishy eyes
Tiny tail
Floppy ears
Heaviest animal.
Guess who?

Rebecca Wilson (10)
Durand Primary School, Caldicot

Guess Who?

Fast runner
Rubbish eater
Rubbish tipper
Rubbish smeller
Naughty squeaker
High jumper
Dark grey
Slow thinker.

Connor McCabe (9)
Durand Primary School, Caldicot

Countdown Of Horses

There are ten horses in the attic
There are nine upon the stairs
There are eight horses watching TV
There are seven sitting on chairs
There are six within the playroom
There are five horses playing ball
There are four doing gymnastics
And three are stuck to the wall
There are two horses on the carpet doing things that horses do
There is one right behind me who is also quiet . . . *boo!*

Daisy Sterry (10)
Durand Primary School, Caldicot

It's Rather Dark In Here

I am writing these poems from inside a cheetah
And it's rather dark in here
So please excuse the handwriting
Which may not be too clear
But this afternoon, by the cheetah's cage
I'm afraid I got too near . . .
And I'm writing these lines from inside a cheetah
And it's rather dark in here.

Adam Price (10)
Durand Primary School, Caldicot

Hamster

It is like a noisy dwarf
It is very fat
It is starting to scratch
It runs from a cat
It is like a rat
It nibbles a lot
It rams food in its mouth.

James Hussey (9)
Durand Primary School, Caldicot

Santa

Santa needs Fanta to help him on his way,
If he doesn't drink he won't be able to ride his sleigh.
Santa please give me some pheasant.
Hopefully I won't get a present.
Oh Santa where have you put Rudolph?
Are you playing golf?
The reindeers are getting tired,
You're being so slow, you're going to get fired.

Zoe Miles (10)
Durand Primary School, Caldicot

Bonfire Night

Bonfire fireworks
Fizz and bang
Catherine wheels spinning
Having fun all around.

Fireworks going zip, bang, bang!
Bonfire going crickle and crack.

And then the night ends with a fizz, bang!
A fizz, zip, bang and a bang!
Crickle and a crack and a big bang.

Hollie Thomas (10)
Durand Primary School, Caldicot

Friends

F riends are awesome,
R eally cool,
I always get along,
E ven when they're gone,
N ever break up,
D on't be afraid,
S o make friends.

Ellie Richards (10)
Durand Primary School, Caldicot

Drama

As I step on the scary stage
Hundreds of people staring at me
I always get my lines wrong
I get nervous singing a song

Should I stay or cry away?
Deciding this all day . . .
The audience are getting bored
They start saying that I drool

As the music begins
I start to sing
The audience clap and cheer
I think right and clear

I get through that horrid song
Shall I always stay on?
I finish the rest of the script
Oh how good I got through it!

Teresa Jones (11)
Durand Primary School, Caldicot

Sparkling Spring

Sparkling spring is on its way,
Sparkling water in the bay.
All the flowers you can see,
Pink, blue and purple, that are lovely.

Everywhere you smell fresh air,
Go on the mountain, but do take care.
Green grass here and there
And time to go to your spring fayre.

The golden sun that shines,
In the wonderful day,
Sparkling spring is on its way,
Sparkling water in the bay.

Shrada Chitlangia (10)
Durand Primary School, Caldicot

It's A Spooky Night

It's a spooky night
When witches come out
Witches with their wands and broomsticks
Very, very ugly indeed
It's a creepy night
When devils come out
With their devil horns on a stick
They come out to get you but are very, very red
It's a creepy night
When ghouls come out
It's a creepy night
When zombies come out
With balls upon their necks
Coming from their graves
It's a spooky night
When ghouls come out.

Katie Webber (10)
Durand Primary School, Caldicot

Mike And Nike's Motorbike

There were two men on a motorbike
They were called Mike and Nike
One day they went out at night
On their motorbike
They set off to Mexico
To see the motorbike show
A man had a fall
And he rolled into a ball
He landed by Mike and Nike
They took him on their motorbike
All the way to the pub.

Joseph St John (10)
Durand Primary School, Caldicot

Dog

Tongue dribbler
Cat hater

Fast chaser
Food gobbler

Cute, cuddly
Soft, cushiony

Rabbit chase
Indian-a-holic

Human jumper
Soft pouncer

Easy sleeper
Chewy muncher

Fast thinker
Easy escaper

Crazy player
Loud barker

Walking lover
Sleeping hugger

Bird chaser
Human racer

Loves me
Always has.

Abbie Cheeseman (9)
Durand Primary School, Caldicot

Rigsby

I once had a dog called Rigsby
He used to play with a Frisbee
He made me laugh when he jumped in the bath
And that's the story of Rigsby.

Brandon Ackerman (10)
Durand Primary School, Caldicot

Food We Eat

F ood is good
O ur food is gorgeous
O ur food we eat
D inner is important

F ood we eat
O ur food is great
O ranges are lush
D inner is amazing

F ood is lovely
O ur food is the best
O ur food is great
D ishes we do

W e eat food
E veryone likes food

E veryone is hungry
A ppetite we all have
T asty and great!

Indya Matthews (8)
Durand Primary School, Caldicot

It's A Teacher

It's big
It's ugly
It's very
Very scary
It's black
It's white
It's very
Very bright
It smells
It tells
It's very
Very nasty.

Joshua Baker (10)
Durand Primary School, Caldicot

The Summertime

The summer lightens your spirit,
It makes you feel so happy,
I wait for it every year,
Look everyone, summer's here.

I like the summer, it makes you feel excited,
It's nice when you can sit and chill.
You can sunbathe and relax
And relax and forget about that horrible stress.
It's nice to sit and wait for a nice tan,
Every day I wake up to the hot glaring sun,
Come on Sam, have some fun.

You can have a lovely barbie,
Oh it's so nice!
It makes your mouth water.

Summer,
I like it because it means you get six weeks off school,
So you get time off, how cool!
Nanny, you rule!

Abigail Lovell (10)
Durand Primary School, Caldicot

My Friends

They care for me when I'm sad
And laugh at me when I'm mad.
Some of them are blonde, some are dark,
But they all glow like a spark.
They are very cool,
They so rule.
They've been there for me all this time,
I do so like this rhyme.

Natalie Bains (9)
Durand Primary School, Caldicot

A World

In my head my world would be
peace with joy,
everyone making new friends.
But when I open up my eyes
and I go to the window it's war,
people killing, people dying,
children hurt, hear them crying.
I can dream can't I!

Jade Upshall (10)
Durand Primary School, Caldicot

My Mother

Ironing hater
Relaxing lover
Soap watcher
Gossip listener
Phone talker
Make-up wearer
Money spender
Washing hater
Chocolate lover.

Victoria Tucker (10)
Durand Primary School, Caldicot

Holiday

Holidays are really fun
You just want to get out and run
There's lots of tasty food
You want to jump up in a groove
I like to ride on rides
And win my friends a prize
You like to watch magic shows
They are good tricks to know.

Rory Bryant (10)
Durand Primary School, Caldicot

Down By The River

Down by the river
Under the dark green trees
I sit and fish and feel the breeze
While listening to the river's powerful flow.

Quick, fast, in and out
The river as a tiger on the prowl
I wait and crouch for a fish
Under the sun by the Tawe.

This beautiful river is the Tawe
Once or twice I see a swan
Look back and it is gone
This reminds me where I am
Yes, Swansea is where I am.

I've seen the fish jump in and out
I love to fish under the bridge
They're all like a big midge
Down by the river.

George R Shepherd (10)
Durand Primary School, Caldicot

Muppet

Kneecap nibbler
Tail wager
Food chomper
Fast eater
Head chopper
Meat muncher
Tree climber
Mice catcher
Hedgehog eater
Me cuddler
Dropper softly.

Paris Gosling (9)
Durand Primary School, Caldicot

The Winter

Snow is like cotton wool
It looks like a fluffy rug
I always go to play in it
I can't wait until winter comes
Hooray, winter is here.

The winter so cold
Let's go and get some snow
We'll go and get our sledge
And go to crash in a hedge
Let's go home to bed.

Tonight it's Christmas Eve
Let's go to bed before we freeze
It's Christmas Day, hooray
Let's go and open some presents
And go to bed before we feed the pheasants.

Lauren O'Leary (10)
Durand Primary School, Caldicot

In A Faraway Land

In an island faraway from here
The people only had one ear

The sky is always blue
They never get the flu

They eat a lot of blocks
And never get chickenpox

There are lots of beaches
But beware of the leeches

This island is great
Well worth the wait.

Daniel Jones (10)
Durand Primary School, Caldicot

My Jumpy, Jimpy Dog

My jumpy, jimpy dog
His name is Jumpy Jim
I call him that because he is so slim
We went to the park
And then he saw a piece of bark
Then he picked up the piece of bark
It was so chewy that his teeth could not get through the bark
Then I took him home and gave him a bone
Then I had to give the vet a phone
With my chewy bone.

Jamie Gough (10)
Durand Primary School, Caldicot

My Alien

My alien's name is Bop
He always comes round with his mop
Cleaning the spaceship all day
He's coming to tea and to play, hooray!
He's always likes me lots and lots
Giving me chocolate tots
After a cup of tea he starts to sing with me
And sing and sing
And the window goes *bang!*
And then he eats an orang-utan!

Jack Jones (10)
Durand Primary School, Caldicot

My Dog

My dog is mad, he runs around the garden chasing aeroplanes
My dog plays football better than the professionals
My dog never stops to rest
My dog is always running riot!
My dog's the *best!*

Emily Millar (10)
Durand Primary School, Caldicot

Winter's Day

Winter is so cold, it always brings a frost,
We usually have some snow when the wind starts to blow.
So come outside and play on the big frosty rides.
So come along and get your hat and coat on,
Then you can bring some big thick kites along.

Winter is here, so cold and bare,
The trees are bare in the fresh lovely air.
So grab some ropes and climb the oak with your big cuddly bear.
Take leaves from the grass and scoop them away in the park,
So that is all from the misty, misty winter days.

Carys Wood (10)
Durand Primary School, Caldicot

Teachers

T eaching the students all year round
E ating at lunchtime, say not a sound
A ny of the students don't do their work
C an go to detention and not a jerk
H aving fun all day long
E veryone can play the bong
R eady to go home, hooray!

Caitlin Richards (10)
Durand Primary School, Caldicot

Grapes

G rapes are nice,
R un in your tummy,
A nd grapes are juicy,
P ie and grapes,
E xciting grapes,
S ee grapes in the shops.

George Pinnell (8)
Durand Primary School, Caldicot

Fruit

F antastic food
R eally nice
U sually healthy
I t is in the fruit bowl
T aste it, don't waste it.

Megan Hardstaff (8)
Durand Primary School, Caldicot

My Lazy Day

I stay in bed till dinner time
I play my CDs and like to mime
I watch movies all day long
I always like to sing a song.

Jessica Purnell (10)
Durand Primary School, Caldicot

Apple

A pples are fruit
P lus they give you energy
P ips grow into mouth-watering apples
L ittle apples on the tree
E xtra juicy - red, yellow, green apples for me.

James Taylor (8)
Durand Primary School, Caldicot

Pasta

P ages of work and then some tea.
A sk if there is seconds.
S top being unhealthy.
T ry being healthy
A nd start being healthy by eating pasta.

Kiaron Tucker (8)
Durand Primary School, Caldicot

Food

F resh food is good for you and it makes you strong.
O ranges are good for you and they are so healthy.
O ranges are juicy and sweet and they are healthy for you.
D on't eat bad stuff, eat good stuff because it makes you healthy.

Lewis Rees (8)
Durand Primary School, Caldicot

Fruit

F ruit is healthy
R ose-red apples
U se fruit for diets
I like fruit
T wo people can share fruit.

Yasmin Chappelle (8)
Durand Primary School, Caldicot

Apple

A n apple
P eople like it
P erfectly good fruit
L ike an apple
E at pieces of fruit every day.

Benjamin McKean Williams (8)
Durand Primary School, Caldicot

Beans

B eans are delicious
E arly morning
A ren't they suspicious
N ot much of a prize
S o yummy.

Lloyd O'Connor (8)
Durand Primary School, Caldicot

Healthy Food

H ave some more fruit
E ating healthy food is so good
A nd you have lots of energy
L ovely, so good, it tastes so good
T hinking of healthy food is so good
H ungry and sweet
Y ou're feeling so sporty with some fruit in you.

F illing your tummy up, it tastes so good
O n your plate it goes
O ften you make
D elicious food.

Shannon Blanchard (8)
Durand Primary School, Caldicot

Bananas

B ananas are yummy, good for your tummy
A t the shops waiting for you
N ice and yellow
A s clean for you
N ow they are right to eat for you
A s you go into the shop, they are looking at you
S aying pick me up to go home.

Shannon May (9)
Durand Primary School, Caldicot

Fruit

F ruit is delicious to eat
R ub out the junk and eat the fruit
U sually good to eat fruit
I am pleased to eat fruit
T o the people who get the fruit off the trees,
thank you for getting them to make us fit.

Niamh Stocker (8)
Durand Primary School, Caldicot

Fish Pizza

F ish on the pizza, yum-yum
I n my tummy it tastes so good
S econds please
H aving this meal cheers me up

P ineapple isn't as good
I prefer fish pizza
Z azam, I think as it comes out the oven
Z ip it up in my bag, I'm hungry
A lovely pizza arrives at the door.

Thomas Jones (8)
Durand Primary School, Caldicot

Nutrition

N othing wrong with fruit and veg
U nhealthy food you eat less
T omatoes are good for you because they're a fruit
R ed apples are great
I n a fruit bowl is full with lovely fruit
T omatoes are great, nice, juicy and red
I n the world we should eat more fruit and veg
O nions are great in vegetable stew
N utritious food is good for you.

Sam Godfrey (9)
Durand Primary School, Caldicot

Potatoes

P recious potatoes
O n the plate ready for you to eat
T aste like fresh daffodils
A sweet, fresh potato
T o veg, to fruit, there is still healthy food
O ur tummies are full of those potatoes.

Joshua Harding (8)
Durand Primary School, Caldicot

Food Delicious

I like mint ice cream,
It looks like a green submarine,
It feels like soft mousse,
It smells like fresh leaves,
It tastes like a delicious sweet.

I hate tomatoes,
They look like rosy cheeks,
They feel like playdoh,
They smell like stuffing,
They taste like wine.

Alisha Roberts (7)
Durand Primary School, Caldicot

Coconuts

C oconuts have got a lot of milk
O n trees they grow
C oconuts will make your mouth water
O f course, they are healthy
N utty brown, hairy coconut
U sually you have to bang them on the table
T aste sweet and good
S uck all the milk out.

Harry Bryant (8)
Durand Primary School, Caldicot

Fruit

F ruit is delicious
R eally nutritious
U nable to hate it
I t really is yummy
T ablespoons full of yummy, scrummy fruit.

Jessica Green (8)
Durand Primary School, Caldicot

I Like, I Hate

I like cheese,
It looks like a yellow blanket,
It feels like a gooey slug,
It smells like smelly feet,
It tastes like a chewy burger.

I hate hamburgers,
They look like hard mud,
They feel like playdoh,
They smell like burnt toast,
They taste like crunchy slugs.

Elliot Thomas (7)
Durand Primary School, Caldicot

Chocolate

C adbury's crème egg
H appy chocolate day
O h I can't resist the smell
C hocolate is catching my lips
O h I love melting chocolate
L ovely chocolate in my mouth
A lovely chocolate cake
T o a lovely chocolate night
E very chocolate bar is mine.

Amelia Reynolds (7)
Durand Primary School, Caldicot

Pasta

P an to plate, it's so great
A ll meaty and fresh
S top being unhealthy
T ry some pasta
A lways delicious and lovely.

Elloise Parker (8)
Durand Primary School, Caldicot

Things I Like, Things I Hate

I like a hamburger,
It looks like a mouth with a tongue,
It feels like some cotton wool,
It smells like a burnt piece of toast,
It tastes like nice feathers.

I hate pizza,
It looks like a car wheel,
It feels like an ice lolly,
It smells like a damp blanket,
It tastes like a broken book.

Harry Jones (7)
Durand Primary School, Caldicot

Red Apple

R ed apple
E ating fruit
D ancing in the bowl

A pple in the night
P eeling it at night
P eeking in night
L ooking in dark
E ating the fruit.

Heather Crispin (8)
Durand Primary School, Caldicot

Grape

G reat fruit all round
R ubbish not to be seen
A pples live in your fruit bowl
P atterns of yummy fruit
E at lots of fruit.

Tristan Cuer (9)
Durand Primary School, Caldicot

Green Apple

G o to the market
R un home fast
E at it all up
E xtremely yummy
N ot much left

A ll juicy and crunchy
P eople like them
P uppies as well
L ike and bite them
E at one every day!

Kelsey-Lee Wright (8)
Durand Primary School, Caldicot

Food/Peas

F ood is great
O n the healthy food
O n a balanced diet
D o you like food?

P eas are nice
E ven water inside
A nd nice
S weet and nice food, oh yeah!

Connor Jones (8)
Durand Primary School, Caldicot

Bacon

B acon is great,
A bsolutely superb,
C an't get enough of it
O h, the taste of bacon
N othing as nice as bacon.

Sam Hooper (7)
Durand Primary School, Caldicot

Food Is Tasty

F ood is great and tasty
O food is tasty, I have to have some
O food is nice, I have to have some
D oing so much, I am hungry

I love it, it's so nice
S avouring it's so nice as it goes down

T aste it, so tasty
A lovely food, it goes down in my tummy
S uch a lovely day for food
T aste is all right with food
Y ou could turn into food.

James Oubridge (8)
Durand Primary School, Caldicot

Oranges

O ranges are sour
R ound and sweet
A ll juicy to eat
N ot the peel
G reat in the middle
E at them every day
S ucking the juices.

Katie Baugh (7)
Durand Primary School, Caldicot

Salmon

S almon in a sandwich
A ll juicy and sweet
L oveliest fish I reckon I could eat
M y favourite sandwich
O n its own or with chips, I don't care
N o other sandwich can compare.

Mathew Stainthorp (8)
Durand Primary School, Caldicot

Chocolate Cake

C reamy chocolate
H ow shall I eat it?
O n top is chocolate icing
C rowded people all around it
O h, so much chocolate makes it nice
L ovely cake in my dreams
A nice try, *mmm . . .*
T alking about it
E verywhere

C utting it is lovely
A chocolate cake tastes nice
K nives are used to cut it
E leven people eat it.

Lucy Hubbard (8)
Durand Primary School, Caldicot

Sweets

S ensational sweets
W aiting for me
E ntertaining for me to see
E verlasting gobstoppers
T asty as candy
S ensational sweets for me to see.

Joseph Voke (8)
Durand Primary School, Caldicot

Fruit

O h, all juicy
R eady for you to eat
A great taste
N o problems
G ood and healthy
E at it quick or it will be gone.

Megan Kemp (8)
Durand Primary School, Caldicot

Delicious Food

I like bacon sandwiches
And I like lots of dips.
I like a lot of pasta
And I like fish and chips.
I like egg sandwiches
And I like swimming in the lake.
I like mashed potato
And I like chocolate cake.

I hate pizza,
It looks like a car wheel,
It feels like burnt toast,
It smells like tomato and cheese,
It tastes like big bricks.

Sam Lloyd (7)
Durand Primary School, Caldicot

My Magic Box

(Based on 'Magic Box' by Kit Wright)

I will put in my box . . .
The cleanest water of all,
The dirtiest earth ever.

I will put in my box . . .
A book but not just any book,
The biggest book in the world,
A TV that nobody has watched.

I will put in my box . . .
A pen that everybody has had,
A pencil that nobody has had.

My box is made out of the rainwater,
A handful of sun,
Its hinges are secrets,
I shall pray in my box.

Mathilda Wellard (9)
St David's CW Primary School, Nr Cowbridge

Sadness Is . . .

Rain dripping on the wet, soggy window.
Watching a 'Lassie' film, when she ran away.
When I see people killing poor animals on TV.
When I am stuck in traffic on a boiling day
And I'm stuck in the hot car.
Me and my sister having an argument
And her putting on the baby videos of us when we were babies.
When you move house and leave school to go to another school.
When I watch the news and see people getting kidnapped.
It sounds like beggars weeping for money.
It is black as the sky at night with lightning
And you cannot get to sleep.

Lowri Allen (8)
St David's CW Primary School, Nr Cowbridge

Happiness

Happiness is yellow like daffodils swaying together,
It tastes like an orange ice pop melting in the sun,
It smells like roses moving slowly in the cold air,
It looks like children playing sweetly,
It sounds like the sea rolling up and down the pebbles,
It feels like the warm wind gently touching your face.

Lauren Bailey (9)
St David's CW Primary School, Nr Cowbridge

Happiness

Happiness is yellow like the cheerful smiles from the sun,
It tastes like a triple-scooped ice cream cone,
It smells like big, bright red, beautiful roses,
It looks like my very best, fantastic volley into the goal,
It sounds like birds singing in the fresh, warm countryside,
It feels like a dog's soft, smooth, velvet ears.

Craig Boxall (8)
St David's CW Primary School, Nr Cowbridge

Sadness Is . . .

Watching the raindrops dripping down my bedroom window
On a black, stormy night.

Falling over on the rock-hard floor
In the playground.

Sitting in the car stuck in the noisy traffic on the way to school.
Coming last in sports day and my dad missing half of it.

Down the beach with my friend Nia in the heavy rain,
Watching the grey sea crashing against the rocky rocks.

Being in a playful fair
And my favourite colour balloon going up in the sky.

Evie Hurford (8)
St David's CW Primary School, Nr Cowbridge

Happiness

Happiness is yellow like the sun smiling on my face.
It tastes like a big juicy strawberry.
It smells like a horse's nose.
It looks like a bunch of red roses.
It sounds like a dog's first bark.
It feels like a velvet sofa.

Emily Davies ·(8)
St David's CW Primary School, Nr Cowbridge

Anger

Anger is silver like lightning speeding through the sky,
It tastes like sour lemons,
It smells like a huge burning fire on Bonfire Night,
It looks like my mum on a Monday morning,
It sounds like raging thunder on a stormy night,
It feels like me scraping my nails down the blackboard.

Kathryn Rees (8)
St David's CW Primary School, Nr Cowbridge

Sadness

Sadness is like the heavy rain pounding on my head.
Rock-hard hailstones crashing on the car window.
Coming last on sports day and then hearing my mum and
dad didn't make it.
Hearing the door slamming behind you and you can't get out.
The feeling of a hard, bumpy stone hidden in the sand.
Losing someone close to you.
Buying a chocolate chip ice cream and dropping it on the sand.
Falling on some hard stones and scraping my knee.
Hearing a teacher scrape her nails down a blackboard.
Seeing lightning strike the muddy black field.

Kimberley Jerwood (8)
St David's CW Primary School, Nr Cowbridge

Anger

Anger is black like a raging thunderstorm,
It tastes like a bitter, sour lemon,
It smells like polish remover,
It looks like a sharp-bladed knife,
It sounds like two people shouting at each other,
It feels like a spiky thorn stuck in your leg
And you can't get it out!

Harriet Richardson (9)
St David's CW Primary School, Nr Cowbridge

Happiness

Happiness is yellow like a bumblebee's fluffy stripes,
It tastes like huge, curly cotton candy,
It smells like a freshly cut orange,
It looks like a shiny conker just fallen,
It sounds like the sea lapping on the sand,
It feels like a brand new pencil in its case.

Harvey Stockford (9)
St David's CW Primary School, Nr Cowbridge

Anger Is . . .

When you tell someone a secret and they deliberately tell
someone else,
When I let my best friend down on a misty, drizzly day,
When my best friend is being bullied by a much older
And bigger boy or girl, it makes me boil red with anger,
When I'm bullied by much older boys and girls,
When I lose a rugby game 10 tries to 0 on a thundery day.
Anger is silver like lightning crashing down and thunder
rumbling away.
Like tips of blazing, fierce, menacing fire licking the air
like a hungry tiger,
Anger sounds like the mighty roar of a fearsome lion coming
closer and closer.

Joseph Davies (8)
St David's CW Primary School, Nr Cowbridge

Anger

Anger is black like a miserable day.
It tastes like bitter lemon in my mouth.
It smells like rotten fish in a stinky freezer.
It looks like a farmer taking the sheep away.
It sounds like thunder crashing in the sky.
It feels like a bush of thorns sticking into me.

Alice Griffiths (9)
St David's CW Primary School, Nr Cowbridge

Anger

Anger is red like the boiling sun,
It tastes like hot, spicy chillies,
It looks like a razor-sharp shark smashing its jaws up and down.
It sounds like my dad kicking his car,
It feels like rough logs just been chopped down.

Harri Jehu (8)
St David's CW Primary School, Nr Cowbridge

Anger

Anger is the colour of a thundering storm blackening the sky,
It smells like burnt chips covered in vinegar,
It looks like a tiger pouncing on the back of a zebra
And a hedgehog in a spiky ball.
It feels like a sharp pin in your finger,
It sounds like a person screaming in your ear
And a baby crying.
It tastes like a slushy, rotten banana
And a spicy hot chilli burning your mouth.

Josie Chivers (9)
St David's CW Primary School, Nr Cowbridge

Sadness Is . . .

When you get a huge, chocolate chip ice cream and drop it,
When you have a friend over
And they have to go because someone has died,
When a black thunderstorm comes on a lovely holiday,
When you make a door stopper and it gets wet
And all the paint drips away,
It sounds like a person crying.

Stephanie Sanderson (8)
St David's CW Primary School, Nr Cowbridge

Sadness

It's turquoise like a balloon going straight in the air.
It tastes like the salty sea.
It smells like black smoke in the dirty air.
It looks like soggy tears pouring out of a person's eye.
It sounds like people shooting an animal
And the animal's cry.
It feels like a hard grey stone hurting your hand.

Miles Davies (8)
St David's CW Primary School, Nr Cowbridge

Anger Poem

Anger tastes like burning curry.
Anger tastes like mushed maggots and onions.

Anger smells like someone who hasn't had a shower like me.
Anger smells like flies around on a pile of dung.

Anger looks like a riot in London.
Anger looks like teachers giving out homework.

Anger sounds like guns being fired.
Anger sounds like windows shattering and people screaming.

Anger feels like mouldy apples.
Anger feels like burning wood in your hands.

Harri Apreda (9)
St David's CW Primary School, Nr Cowbridge

Sadness

Sadness is grey like slithering raindrops sliding down my window
on my birthday,
It tastes like an over-burnt spicy chicken burger,
It smells like gone-off cheese,
It looks like thousands of children crying somberly,
It sounds like bombs falling viciously down in World War II,
It feels like falling on a rock-hard floor.

Liam Sloan (8)
St David's CW Primary School, Nr Cowbridge

Anger

Anger is red like bright, gooey paint,
It tastes like hot burnt chilli and you want to get water,
It smells like fresh tyre marks on the road,
It looks like a farmer killing a chick by breaking its legs,
It sounds like an aeroplane crashing down,
It feels like a rotten bone in my hands.

Tom Roberts (8)
St David's CW Primary School, Nr Cowbridge

Happiness

Happiness feels like silk
And newly-born lambs in green flowering fields.

Happiness sounds like the sea coming up
The pebbly beach and a baby's laugh.

Happiness looks like a beautiful sunset
And swimming in the blue sea.

Happiness smells like flowers
And melted chocolate.

Happiness tastes like sweets
And ice cream.

Amelia Glanville (9)
St David's CW Primary School, Nr Cowbridge

Anger

Anger is red like a blazing fire,
It tastes like a chilli burning in my mouth,
It smells like smoke from a huge fire,
It looks like a tiger pouncing,
It sounds like thunder hitting a tree,
It feels like walking through a thorny bush.

Emme Srinivas (8)
St David's CW Primary School, Nr Cowbridge

Happiness

Happiness is red like the beautiful roses gleaming in the sun.
It tastes like a big, fat, juicy orange.
It smells like bluebells glistening in the woods.
It looks like a blue sea bobbing in the hot sun.
It sounds like a cute dog barking.
It feels like soft puppies sleeping.

Scott Thomas (9)
St David's CW Primary School, Nr Cowbridge

Frightening

F inding a stone stuck in your bone.
R iding your bike through the deep dark forest.
I n a mansion on your own.
G etting punched by my big brother Boris.
H elicopters landing right on top of you.
T urtles getting run over.
E verybody running over you.
N ine footballs crashing into the net
I n a rock cave where it is pitch-black.
N owhere to hide from the big fat giant.
G oats headbutting and biting me.

Tom Owen (9)
St David's CW Primary School, Nr Cowbridge

Anger

Anger is red like fresh lava,
It tastes like a big maggot,
It smells like blood from an injured cat,
It looks like a bird falling from the sky,
It sounds like someone screaming,
It feels like a thorny cactus.

Thomas Whitehouse (8)
St David's CW Primary School, Nr Cowbridge

Happiness

Happiness is yellow like the smiling sunflower.
It tastes like a chocolate chip ice cream.
It smells like the freshly cut field.
It looks like a glittery rosebush.
It sounds like bright bluebirds singing.
It feels like scoring a fantastic goal in the Champion's League.

Michael Milani (8)
St David's CW Primary School, Nr Cowbridge

Happiness

Happiness, happiness,
It looks like a peach in the middle of the sea.
Happiness looks like red strawberry jam.

It feels like the softest sand in the world,
It tastes like the sweetest food.

And the colour of happiness is red,
Happiness smells like fresh-picked raspberries.

Jac Apreda (9)
St David's CW Primary School, Nr Cowbridge

Sadness

It tastes like gone-off custard and mouldy bread.
It smells like mud and a cold bath.
It looks like thousands of monsters coming this way
And lots of people getting hurt.
It sounds like someone playing a squeaky instrument
And rain falling on the ground.
It feels like squidgy goo and smelly hair gel.
Its colours are black and red.

Harry Massie (9)
St David's CW Primary School, Nr Cowbridge

Anger

Anger tastes like spicy curry
Anger smells like vinegar and chopped onions
Anger feels like hot cheesy pizza
Anger is the colour of a stormy black night
Anger sounds like banging drums
And a herd of elephants stamping down the road
Anger looks like red-hot fire and a very angry face.

Leo Bailey (9)
St David's CW Primary School, Nr Cowbridge

Hallowe'en

The big dark night,
Watch out it'll give you a fright.
If you see the witch in the sky,
Look up, don't be shy.

Hallowe'en on the 31st of October.
Hallowe'en with evil pumpkin faces.
Hallowe'en, when sweets fill up your bag.

The Devil spooks you out of your skin,
You scream, you can't do anything.

Nia Patel (9)
St David's CW Primary School, Nr Cowbridge

Love

Love tastes of fizzy lemonade
And sweet, sweet honey.
It smells of beautiful roses
And sweet candy.
It looks like a river flowing
And trees blowing in the wind.
It feels like a heron
And doves cooing.
You can hear the sound of harps playing and violins.

Ellie Cridland (9)
St David's CW Primary School, Nr Cowbridge

A Worry Poem

Worry tastes like lumpy custard.
Worry looks like thick grey mist.
Worry smells like a mouldy banana left behind.
Worry sounds like a hundred drums slowly beating.
Worry feels like you just dropped a vase that cost £100.

Ben Crosby (9)
St David's CW Primary School, Nr Cowbridge

Christmas

C hristmas morning's really fun.
H oping Father Christmas has eaten his bun.
R unning down the stairs to play with my new toys.
I gnoring my brother, because he makes all the noise.
S ilently waiting for my parents to wake.
T esting if my mum walks downstairs like a snake.
M erry Christmas, shout my friends.
A lex, my mate, wishes that Christmas never ends.
S o that is why Christmas is the best time of year.

Matthew Howells (9)
St David's CW Primary School, Nr Cowbridge

Best Friends

It tastes like friends together all day long.
It smells like friends with lovely roses just for you and me.
It sounds like people laughing all day long.
It smells like a rose with so many friends for everyone to play with.
It makes a very happy cake, so many people can eat the cake.
It's so happy and you can make new friends.
It feels like everyone's so happy
And you just want to be happy for everyone in the world.

Dominique Mears (9)
St David's CW Primary School, Nr Cowbridge

My World

My world is big and round and full of lots of people,
It's hot and cold and busy and makes me very dizzy.
Places to go, people to see, my world is wonderful to me.

My world is great, my world is fab,
But sometimes it makes me mad.
It makes me mad in so many ways I can't say,
I love my world anyway, even though it's a pain sometimes.

Georgina Beswick (10)
St David's CW Primary School, Nr Cowbridge

The Hunt

Jaws snapping,
Tails slapping,
Claws scratching,
Teeth matching,
Legs flashing,
Almost crashing,

Rabbits hopping,
Never stopping,
Deer stamping,
Teeth clamping,

Guns shooting,
Owls hooting,
Hearing the bang,
Showing the fangs,
Hoping to live,
Never to forgive,

Blood spurting, the hunters lurking!

Bryony Roberts (9)
St David's CW Primary School, Nr Cowbridge

Happiness

It feels like someone has burst out with laughter.
It looks like pink tree trunks and bright blue leaves.
It sounds like a monkey giggling as it swings from tree to tree.
It smells like flowers picked from the garden.
It tastes like a fairy cake that has just been baked.

Melissa Hamilton (9)
St David's CW Primary School, Nr Cowbridge

War

Walking onto the battlefield,
Taking out your shield,
Walking into war with your weapons,
Hearing your opponents beckon.

War is a dreadful thing,
Leaving the dead to sing,
Nobody likes war,
It's like eating an apple core.

In the war,
The worst place to be,
Everyone is sad,
Can't you see!

Who likes war?
The Devil of course.
War is the worst thing ever,
Like the yuckiest sauce.

Jack Anthony Scott-Coombes (9)
St David's CW Primary School, Nr Cowbridge

Fear

Fear tastes like damp, bumpy, cold, mushy peas.
Fear looks like a lumpy monster and trees with no leaves.
Fear smells like a dark, lonely dustbin with a tramp inside.
Fear sounds like thunder in a storm and windows in a
hurricane shattering.

Fear feels lonely and weak.

Joanna Wilkins (9)
St David's CW Primary School, Nr Cowbridge

Animals

Horses are nice soft friends,
They can keep your secrets,
You can ride your furry friends,
They won't mind a bit.

Dogs are cute and warm,
Puppies a bundle of fun,
Can you cope with this whirlwind?
Of course you can, it might be fun.

Cats are cute but don't be misled,
Cats are killers, well, only sometimes.
You can play with a kitten,
They are playful and friendly.

Rabbits with their floppy ears,
They're funny, friendly and playful.
If you have a rabbit,
You'll have plenty of fun and laughs.

Emily Manogg (9)
St David's CW Primary School, Nr Cowbridge

Chocolate!

Chocolate is lush.
Chocolate is cool.
Chocolate makes me swim in a swimming pool.

Chocolate is sweet.
Chocolate is yummy.
Chocolate rumbles in my tummy.

Chocolate is hard.
Chocolate is brown.
I sneak chocolate in my gown!

I love chocolate!

Nicky Griffiths (9)
St David's CW Primary School, Nr Cowbridge

My Magic Potion

In my cauldron I am going to mix . . .
A sliced, dead, maggoted fox, once full of tricks,
A slimy, dead, smelly skunk and cows' guts raw,
A fat, grimy frog and a human's jaw,
Ten live worms, a fat bat's wings,
A buzzard's head and a wasp's sting.

Hippo saliva and cat's pee,
I'll mix this all up with glee.
The teacher will drink this from her cup
Enjoying every sup.

Her skin will burn brown and she'll grow some hair
She will start to howl in the air.
Her face will turn into a dog-like jaw
Her hands and feet will turn into sharp paws.

She will become a *werewolf!*

Dylan Edwards (8)
St Joseph's Primary School, Galbally, Dungannon

The Writer Of This Poem Is . . .

(Based on 'The Writer of this Poem' by Roger McGough)

The writer of this poem is . . .
As clumsy as a rock.
As funny as a clown.
As cool as a cat.
As smart as a computer.
As shy as a new person.
As high as a lamp post.
As boring as a teacher.
As bright as the sun.

Oliver Tally (9)
St Joseph's Primary School, Galbally, Dungannon

The Writer Of This Poem Is . . .

(Based on 'The Writer of this Poem' by Roger McGough)

As fast as a jet
As small as a pet
As lazy as a monkey
As crazy as a lion
As light as a feather
As chatty as a bird
As strong as a brick
As skinny as a stick
As shy as a monkey
As noisy as a donkey.

Daniel Kerr (8)
St Joseph's Primary School, Galbally, Dungannon

My Magic Potion

I will mix in my cauldron . . .
Sliced pigs' snouts, rats' tails,
Smashed-up slimy slugs and a hard-backed snail,
Chopped lamb's liver
And fish from the river.
Mixed with the blood of a cow so red
And throw in some dry bread.
Teacher will turn into a cat
And look so ugly and fat.

Liam Rafferty
St Joseph's Primary School, Galbally, Dungannon

A Limerick

There was an old man called Fred,
He liked to sleep in his bed.
He never went out,
He just picked his snout,
That was the story of Fred.

Emma Barr (10)
St Joseph's Primary School, Galbally, Dungannon

My Magic Potion

In my cauldron I will put a . . .
Chopped donkey's intestines, so nasty,
Frog's legs, so green
And the hairiest badger's snout you've ever seen.
I'll mix with blood of a cow
And the wee of a sow.
The teacher will cover with hair
And fall off her chair,
She will also change into a dog - so dark
And do nothing, only bark.

Colm McAleer (9)
St Joseph's Primary School, Galbally, Dungannon

Autumn

In autumn nights
The fires burn bright.

The sheep are now down from the hills
While the cattle find standing in the shed no thrill.

The leaves turn red, brown and yellow
And the weather is no longer mellow.

We now have warmer clothes to wear
And on our wet roads have to take more care.

Enda McAleer (9)
St Joseph's Primary School, Galbally, Dungannon

A Limerick

There was an old man called Jimmy,
He had a son called Timmy.
He got hit by lots of cars,
And could see lots of stars,
And that was the end of Timmy.

Ciaran McKeever (11)
St Joseph's Primary School, Galbally, Dungannon

The Magic Potion

Double, double,
Boil and trouble,
Stir in a scorpion's sting
And watch the brew bubble.

See my cauldron overflowing
With the slimiest slugs
And I'll add for flavour
Some wriggling bugs.

Deep in the forest lies
My cauldron of magic,
Creating a potion to cause
Something terribly tragic.

For all the children who
Love lemonade,
Will soon be sipping my potion
At the Hallowe'en parade!

They'll start to choke
As their faces turn blue
And they'll shrivel up into tiny ants,
As they sneeze,
'Aitchoo!'

Áine McCaughey (9)
St Joseph's Primary School, Galbally, Dungannon

Autumn

Autumn time is here,
Some of the animals disappear.
By the fire we like to sit and warm our toes
While outside the cold north wind blows.
Some birds have flown away
And some birds from the north have come to stay.
Now we have longer nights
The red, orange and yellow leaves are a pretty sight.

Lelia Gormley (9)
St Joseph's Primary School, Galbally, Dungannon

My Magic Potion

Ten frogs' eyelids,
Three newts' ears,
Cows' chopped guts,
And snakes' tears.
Weasels' tails
And six bats' eyes,
Five fat slugs,
And ten dead flies.
Into my cauldron I will put this
And then mix with dogs' vomit and elephant wee.
I'll chant *wibble wobble*
And hopefully teacher will gobble,
She will shrink down small
So that she will hardly be seen at all.
Her bones will turn into stones,
She will be as hard as a rock,
And will never again be able to wear a frock.

Kieran Holland (8)
St Joseph's Primary School, Galbally, Dungannon

The Writer Of This Poem Is . . .

(Based on 'The Writer of this Poem' by Roger McGough)

The writer of this poem is . . .
As tall as a tree
As bad as can be
As boring as a teacher
As heavy as a brick
As lively as a football player
As strong as a wrestler
As funny as a clown
As bright as the sun
As lazy as a pig
As loud as a radio
As fast as a car
And as crazy as a frog.

Tiarnan O'Neill (9)
St Joseph's Primary School, Galbally, Dungannon

The Magic Box

(Based on 'Magic Box' by Kit Wright)

I will put in the box . . .
A baby's first words
The cry of a newborn baby
The feel of a baby's hand in mine.

I will put in the box . . .
The chatter of my pencil case
A sip of the water from Cappagh Reservoir
The sting of an electric eel.

I will put in the box . . .
The first joke from my grandad
A pot of gold in my hand
All the colours of the rainbow bursting to life.

My box is fashioned from . . .
Love, happiness and pixie dust
With mermaids dancing, stars and diamonds on the lid
And fairies laughing in the corners
Its hinges are the fingers of princesses.

I shall sail around the world in my magic box
I will touch the sun and slide down rainbows
Then I will swim with dolphins in the Indian Ocean
And go back in time to meet Leonardo da Vinci.

Laura Kane (9)
St Joseph's Primary School, Galbally, Dungannon

Autumn

In autumn warmer clothes we have to wear
And on the wet and foggy roads take care.
The farmer is busy feeding his animals in the shed,
We watch the leaves turn yellow, brown and red.
The fallen leaves litter the ground,
But now no flowers can be found.

Connor Donnelly (8)
St Joseph's Primary School, Galbally, Dungannon

The Magic Box

(Based on 'Magic Box' by Kit Wright)

I will put in the box . . .
The sound of a tractor roaring up a hill
A spark from a firework in the dark night sky
The feel of a fingertip gently wiping a tear from my face.

I will put in the box . . .
The sound of laughter and cheers
The taste of corn on the cob with melting butter
The smoke from the exhaust of a Mercedes Benz.

I will put in the box . . .
The largest football in the world
The happiness I felt when Tyrone won the All Ireland
My favourite football strip.

My box is fashioned from aluminium steel
With footballs and fireworks on the lid
And all my secrets in the corners
Its hinges are rusty and squeak.

I shall surf the high seas in my magic box
And use my great strength to knock the school down
With one punch of my fist.

Brian McNulty (10)
St Joseph's Primary School, Galbally, Dungannon

Hallowe'en Hotpot

Skinny tail of a hairy rat,
Postman's head and his leather hat,
The tail of a stout dog,
The green foot of a strangled frog,
A stupid, ginger, bulky cat,
The brain of a speared bat.

Tiarnan Rafferty (11)
St Joseph's Primary School, Galbally, Dungannon

The Magic Potion

In the deep, dark forest I will cook my magic potion,
To stir up trouble for all teachers.
I will add a scorpion sting and the rotting bones of a skeleton.
Next I will throw in a dead frog's legs and the trunk of an elephant.
Then I will add Rooney's brain, the head of a zombie and a vulture's claw.
I'll blend in the howl of a banshee, the sharp fangs of Dracula
And a lizard's tail
And lastly I'll drop in a dead swordfish, using the sword to stir up my potion.
Now my potion is ready, it is all gloomy, slimy and green,
It will add a garlic flavour to the soup from the canteen.
When the teachers' tummies are full, they'll start to wriggle and squirm about,
Then they'll start squeaking and scratching and brown hairs will spout.
They'll shrink into small balls of fur and stare with mad red eyes,
And they will go crazy as they turn into fat hairy rats,
To everyone's surprise!

Thomas McCool (9)
St Joseph's Primary School, Galbally, Dungannon

My Magic Potion

Into my cauldron I am going to put in ten rotten eggs
And twenty slimy frogs' legs
A kipper so yellow
Two squashed bananas so yellow
I'll mix with elephants' dribble
And some cats' piddle
I'll change my teacher into a frog
And she'll think she is in the bog
She'll grow two back legs
Lay lots of eggs
Two bulging eyes will pop
And away she will hop.

Dearbhla Nugent (9)
St Joseph's Primary School, Galbally, Dungannon

The Magic Box

(Based on 'Magic Box' by Kit Wright)

I will put in the box . . .
A baby's first cry
The touch of a smooth hedgehog
An elephant with tiny ears.

I will put in the box . . .
The teardrop from a basking shark
An emerald-green sky and sky-blue grass
A sip from the crystal-blue water from Altmore Pond.

I will put in the box . . .
The screech of an elephant flying across the sky
The trumpet of a bird swimming across the sea
The Tyrone fans' cheers when Mulligan scored that wonder goal.

My box is fashioned from steel and gold
With stars on the lid and tissue paper in the corners
Its hinges are butterfly wings.

I shall bungee jump into the deepest sea in the world
In the magic box and slide down the biggest wave
In the Irish Sea.

Gareth Kelly (9)
St Joseph's Primary School, Galbally, Dungannon

Hallowe'en Hotpot

A long winding tail of a monkey
The hoof of an old grey donkey
An eye of a horrible newt
A foot of a baby so cute
The slimy tongue of an icky frog
The snotty nose of a live hog
The scaly skin of a dead fish
(You would not want that on a dish)
The venomous teeth of a snake
In the witch's cauldron boil and bake.

Niall McCaughey (11)
St Joseph's Primary School, Galbally, Dungannon

Magic Potion

A sliced elephant's trunk tastes sweet
Sharks' eyeballs, what a treat
Bats' eyelids and a pig's snout
A rhino's bladder and a smelly trout
Mix together round and round
With as much elephant as can be found
Then the magic words I will say
Hoping my teacher a mouse will stay
She will shrink to the ground
And a squeak will be her sound
She will be covered with grey hair too
And a pink nose will shine through
She will be a tiny mouse
And not be welcome in any house.

Aidan Loughran (9)
St Joseph's Primary School, Galbally, Dungannon

My Magic Potion

Six dead ducks, five cats' skins,
A disgusting rabbit and a fat pumpkin,
Some crocodile teeth so shiny,
Ten eels so slimy,
With slimy spider juice
And the milk of a noose.
When my teacher drinks my potion
She will no longer have a notion.
She'll start to bray
And grow a hairy coat of grey.
Her feet and hands will become hooves
On which she can put iron shoes.
She will become a donkey,
So don't mistake her for a monkey.

Callum Kelly (8)
St Joseph's Primary School, Galbally, Dungannon

My Magic Potion

Into my cauldron I shall put . . .
The brains of a baby ox and a sly fox's gut.
Add the blood of a goat and the eyeballs of a fish,
To make this a tasty, revolting dish.
Add the vomit of a dog then stir in some lice,
The head of a shark, a dead lizard and all things nice,
Then finally I'll add the slimy tongue of a toad,
Bluebottles' poo and a rotten cheese mould.
Now the potion is ready . . .
And I'll add a drop in Miss McAleer's tea,
So she'll never ever give us homework again . . .
Now this I gotta see!

John Rafferty (9)
St Joseph's Primary School, Galbally, Dungannon

My Magic Potion

In my cauldron I am going to mix . . .
Fox's teeth so sharp and white,
A hippo's tongue, oh what a sight.
Lots of frogs' legs and a person's foot,
Twenty wiggly worms and a worn-out boot.
Mix with two full buckets of vomit
As I chant 'wibble wobble gamit'.
When the teacher sniffs her nose will pierce
She will become a *lion* so fierce!
Her body will be covered with yellow and orange hair,
On her neck a heavy mane will grow so fair.
A great big brown tail will come out,
Everyone around her will shout!

Blaithin Rafferty (8)
St Joseph's Primary School, Galbally, Dungannon

The Magic Box

(Based on 'Magic Box' by Kit Wright)

I will put in my box . . .
Smelly Christmas spice
And sit up and eat chicken and rice.

I will put in my box . . .
A chicken called Peg
With only one little leg
And a black sea and a blue sky at night.

I will put in my box . . .
A knight in shining armour
Coming to rescue a princess
In a tiny tower surrounded by dragons.

My box is fashioned from marbles and rubies
And the light of a shooting star in the corners
Its hinges are sea lions
Playing with a beach ball in the sea.

I shall swim in the deep blue sea
The small Atlantic ocean where birds
And animals sing sweetly in the air
And that is my magic box sweet, soft and clear.

Lauren McCrory (9)
St Joseph's Primary School, Galbally, Dungannon

A Limerick

I have a friend called Billy
He is really, really silly,
He scored a top corner goal,
Then his jumper got stole
And that made his belly very chilly.

Niall Carberry (10)
St Joseph's Primary School, Galbally, Dungannon

The Magic Box

(Based on 'Magic Box' by Kit Wright)

I will put in my box . . .
The sound of a flickering fire
And a treasure that has never been found.

I will put in my box . . .
The sound of a tiger prowling up in the sky,
The taste of a blackberry flying high,
The cheesy moon ever so small.

I will put in my box . . .
The smell of newly-cut grass,
The sound of the crashing waves going by,
The taste of the ice cream melting in my mouth.

My box is fashioned from the finest silver of them all
With the biggest cobwebs in the world on the lid
And unicorns and butterflies in the corners.
Its hinges are purple with flowers and spots.

I shall play on swings and slides
And I shall have fairies in it.
I shall have a small horse in it
And a pink limo.

Laura-Jayne Donnelly (9)
St Joseph's Primary School, Galbally, Dungannon

A Limerick

Once there was a girl called Kelly,
Who ate loads of garlic jelly.
No one liked the smell,
That Kelly did repel,
So Kelly gave up on the jelly.

Clodagh Rafferty (10)
St Joseph's Primary School, Galbally, Dungannon

My Magic Potion

I'm making a big potion with lots of disgusting things,
I'll need a barrel first, then I'll add some waxy bat wings,
In goes a slimy, slippery slug
And the ear of a goblin and a hairy cow's lug.
I'll pop in the bushy tail of a cunning red fox
And stir in the smelliest, stinkiest socks.
I'll beat the mixture round and round
And I'll add a daddy-long-legs that I've just pinched off the ground.
Now it's ready, I'll have to give it to Mrs Quinn in Primary 5,
I hear she likes her chocolate, so I'll inject it with the potion
And see how she thrives.
She'll reach into her drawer some day where she keeps her
Chocolate store
And she'll think it so tasty that she'll gobble up more and more.
And when she bites into the twentieth chocolate chunk
She'll start to double in size and turn into the Incredible Green Hulk!

Adam Arthurs (9)
St Joseph's Primary School, Galbally, Dungannon

My Hideout

The musty smell of the decaying dead leaves,
As they lie damp under the wide tree, whiffs up my nose.

The sight of my dog, old and scruffy,
Snuffling in the undergrowth
And the ageing trees with their massive branches,
Shading me from the sun fill me with joy.

I hear a hungry dog barking like mad in the distance,
The crunching twigs under my feet
And the rustling leaves overhead.

The touch of the mossy, wet bark of a tree
And the loose damp soil in my shoes annoys me.

I feel the leaves as they gently tap my face
And the secure shade of the tree as it keeps me hid.

Colin Campbell (9)
St Joseph's Primary School, Galbally, Dungannon

My Favourite Place

The theme park

The sweetness of the popcorn, candyfloss tickles my tongue.
The screaming of excited and terrified people pollutes the air.
The whirling rides and the looping roller coaster dazzle my eyes.
The fast-food stall, the oil of machines' fumes attacks my nostrils.
The tight-gripping, reassuring hand of Mum when we're on the
roller coaster.

Mark Quinn (8)
St Joseph's Primary School, Galbally, Dungannon

Hallowe'en Hotpot

A bloody liver from a hairy dog,
A slimy tongue of a green, smelly frog,
A fluffy tail of a lazy fat cat,
A waxy ear of a skinny, fast rat,
The horrible odour of a skunk,
The terrible blood brain of a punk,
The yellow teeth of a giant donkey,
The skinny bones of a jumpy monkey.

Alicia McGuigan (10)
St Joseph's Primary School, Galbally, Dungannon

Love

Love is going to Leeds.
Love is in God's hands.
Love is beautiful.
Love is magical.
Love is my family.
Love is love.
Most of all, love is Christmas.

Mustafa Yavuz (8)
St Mary's RC Primary School, Edinburgh

My Rabbit

My rabbit is as black as a cat,
Just fancy that!
She's as dark as the night
And she's always right,
Because she leaves the food she doesn't like.
She has a hutch
Which she doesn't like much,
But she spends her time outside.
She nibbles the plants bit by bit,
But carrots are her favourite.

Tallulah McCowan Hill (8)
St Mary's RC Primary School, Edinburgh

My Teacher Is A Monster!

My teacher is a monster,
She gobbles the children up.
My teacher is a vampire,
She sucks the children's blood.
My teacher is an alien,
She probes our minds so that we do our work!

Declan Logan (8)
St Mary's RC Primary School, Edinburgh

Animal Poem

Some animals are cute and some are ugly.
I like dogs and bunnies,
Monkeys and rhinos and kangaroos too.
Animals are everywhere in a zoo,
Snakes and deer are all right too,
Animals everywhere in a zoo!

Stephanie McAdam (7)
St Mary's RC Primary School, Edinburgh

Happiness

Happiness is like the stars
Happiness is playing the guitar
Happiness to me is red, blue, green and yellow
Happiness is in your dreams
Happiness is as blue as the sea
Happiness is as green as the grass
Happiness is as red as a rose
Happiness is as yellow as the sun that shines today
And will be for evermore,
But most of all, happiness is you!

Sophie Benson (8)
St Mary's RC Primary School, Edinburgh

Happiness

Happiness is life and grand
Happiness is good and thankful
Happiness is glad and hopeful
Happiness is peace and quiet
Happiness is good and thankful
Happiness is the heart.

Fraser Murray (9)
St Mary's RC Primary School, Edinburgh

Feelings

Happiness is love.
Happiness is bright.
Happiness is happiness.
Happiness is sharing,
Most of all, happiness is joyful.

Harry Robinson (8)
St Mary's RC Primary School, Edinburgh

My Best Teacher

My best teacher loves drinking tea,
She goes back home at half past three.
She boils the kettle for her feet
And makes her house smell like cheese.
She's a bit of a devil
And she's called Miss Reville,
But she's the funniest teacher of all
And she's the best at playing ball
Which is hard for me
And she's the best teacher for you and me!

Marisha Worsnop (8)
St Mary's RC Primary School, Edinburgh

I Think My Teacher Is . . .

I think my teacher is a witch
because she has a cat.

I think my teacher is a ghost
because she is so spooky.

I think my teacher is a vampire
because she's about to eat me up!

Victoria Macfie (8)
St Mary's RC Primary School, Edinburgh

My Teacher is A . . .

My teacher is a ghost,
She scares the class away.

My teacher is a bad teacher,
She drives the head teacher away.

My teacher is a vampire
Because she sucks the children's blood!

Callum Hand (8)
St Mary's RC Primary School, Edinburgh

I Think My Dad Is A Ballerina

I think
my dad is a ballerina,
it's not
just . . .
because he goes
to work
in a
leotard,
and it's
not just . . .
because
he
dances to
strange music.

But . . . it's because he
goes
bonkers up
on
stage.

Garrett Sayle (8)
St Mary's RC Primary School, Edinburgh

I Think My Teacher Is An Alien

It's not just that she rides in a spaceship to school
And that she has a pet bull that destroys the school.

She talks very funny and she uses strange money.
She killed a little bunny and ate it with honey.

That's why I think my teacher is an alien!

Lewis Lindsay (7)
St Mary's RC Primary School, Edinburgh

Happiness

Happiness is colourful.
Happiness is friendship.
Happiness is like a rainbow.
Happiness is helping other children.
Happiness is fantastic.
Happiness is lovely.
Happiness is bright.
Happiness is happiness.
Most of all, happiness is when somebody plays with me.

Simrin Singh (7)
St Mary's RC Primary School, Edinburgh

Scared

Scared is when the ghosts come out
Scared is when wolves howl
Scared is a dark colour like black, grey or brown
Scared is when you tell ghost stories to your friends
Most of all, scared is when the door creaks open
Scared is always scared.

Oliver Rhodes (8)
St Mary's RC Primary School, Edinburgh

A Big Silly Boy

Once there was a boy named Dan,
He was a big Beano fan,
He was such a menace
And looked like Dennis,
Playing tricks on his silly old gran.

Louis Milne (8)
St Mary's RC Primary School, Edinburgh

Happiness

Happiness is joyful.
Happiness is bright and shiny.
Happiness is when you see a rainbow.
Happiness is when I hug my mum and dad.
Happiness is when I hug my puppy called Jack.
Happiness is when I see the sun shining.
Happiness is happiness when I go swimming.
Most of all, happiness is helping my mum.

Priyank Venkatesh (8)
St Mary's RC Primary School, Edinburgh

Happiness

Happiness is joyful
Happiness is shiny
Happiness is love
Happiness is friendly
Happiness is funny
Happiness is fun
Most of all, happiness is a family.

Melania Cilia (8)
St Mary's RC Primary School, Edinburgh

Happiness

Happiness is like the colours of the rainbow.
Happiness is like friendship.
Happiness is like lots and lots of sleep.
Happiness is like Christmas time and presents.
Happiness is playing games with your friends.
Happiness is like a star in the night sky.
Happiness is having nice friends.
Happiness is happiness,
But most of all, happiness is love.

Michael McDermid (8)
St Mary's RC Primary School, Edinburgh

Love

Love is love and always will be.
It's as sneaky as a cat.
It travels in slow motion.
It will jump on you just like that!

Indira Fernando (7)
St Mary's RC Primary School, Edinburgh

Mutiny

There stands the captain at the bow of the ship,
His long, black, wiry beard, flying in the wind,
Stretching the skin on his cracked bottom lip,
And his bloodthirsty mind's intentions showing.
His pale face wanting more spillage of gore and guts,
His crew, bloodthirsty too,
His eyes, hazel and evil and
The jewels on his best clothes, clouded in the rain.

The ship they were chasing, lot smaller than theirs,
But inside himself, the captain wanted more bloodshed and chaos,
Little did he know that the crew planned a battle,
They hoped it to end in the captain's demise.
That night in his cabin,
The captain slept soundly,
In crept the crew,
On with an eye-patch and a peg-leg,
He whispered harshly,
That they should just tie him up so he could die a slow and suffering death.

In the dawn when the captain awoke, he could not get up,
He pulled out a penknife and cut through the rope,
He tried to calculate the men he could trust,
He did not think there was such a man,
So he cut his own flesh and dropped the blood into the sea,
Up swam the sharks, hungry as ever,
Then suddenly, before anyone saw, he threw himself to his death.

Grace Sherratt (10)
Scoraig Primary School, Garve

Myself

I'm nobody else,
I am in my own body, myself,
I think only for me,
Who am I? Do you know?

I think for nobody else,
I am only in myself,
And know my own body,
I'm me now, who are you?

I am myself, nobody else,
I think only for me,
I'm in my own body,
Do you know who I am?

Rhiona Brudenell (10)
Scoraig Primary School, Garve

The Grey Pussy

There was a grey pussy from Fife
Who had a very wonderful life
He lived in a house
With a little black mouse
And begged her to become his new wife.

Emma Fraser (10)
Stratherrick Primary School, Inverness

Rhiannon

There was once a pretty young girl called Rhiannon,
She worked at the circus and got shot out of a cannon,
It hurt a lot
When she got shot,
That poor little young girl called Rhiannon!

Izzy Parrott (9)
Stratherrick Primary School, Inverness

The Wizard's Brew

Into my brew I will put . . .
A young baby and an old coot

An old man's pants and Santa's coat
Followed by blood of a goat

Inky-pinky, I'm very stinky
Hang on, I need a thinky

Three dead rats and four dead bees
And then some disgusting hair fleas

Some clown hair and vampire teeth
With some already eaten beef

Inky-pinky, I'm very stinky
Hang on, I need a thinky

One hairy toe and some nose hairs
And then some five-year-old rotten pears

And don't forget three pints of goo
Mixed up with a fat man's poo

Inky-pinky, I'm very stinky
Hang on, I need a thinky!

Fraser Macpherson (11)
Stratherrick Primary School, Inverness

My Dad

He's very small,
Wide as a hall.
He has a big belly,
He watches telly.
He has grey hair,
When we play games he's always fair.
His jokes are funny,
His nose is runny.
When I kiss him his beard's like sandpaper,
He always has a caper!

Hannah Tweedlie (11)
Stratherrick Primary School, Inverness

Abracadabra And Hocus Pocus

Abracadabra and hocus pocus
Shut up now, I'm trying to focus

A young ghost's head
And a spider's web

Abracadabra and hocus pocus
Shut up again, I'm still trying to focus

An old wizard's mother
A big blood smother

Abracadabra and hocus pocus
Shut up again, I'm still trying to focus

The heart of the sea
And a bumblebee

Abracadabra and hocus pocus
Shut up now, I'm still trying to focus

The water of the loo
And the body of *you!*

Naomi Chattington (8)
Stratherrick Primary School, Inverness

Witch's Brew

Into my cauldron I will put
Leg of lamb and a bowl of soot.

Wing of bird and head of frog
The skin of dog with some fog.

A stolen hen, a mouldy sock
And for good flavour, a prison lock.

Hocus pocus
Be quiet now, I'm trying to focus!

One dead bird, a stolen shoe
And a pint of poo and head of *you!*

Hannah-Kelly Tay (9)
Stratherrick Primary School, Inverness

Witch's Brew

Into my cauldron now I will add
A dead man's foot and a waxed hairy pad

Old men's socks and dirty jeans
A rotten egg and cold baked beans

Abracadabra, it must last
I will feed it to the children, speedy, fast

One dead fly and a wild wasp's sting
The eye of a sheep and the snot that I bring

A stolen jewel and a mouldy rock
And, for good flavour, a gross slimy sock

Abracadabra, it must last
I will feed it to the children, speedy, fast

Wing of a bird and head of a cat
Remember to add the claw of a bat

Don't forget a pint of poo
And let's just add the blood from *you*

Abracadabra, it must last
I will feed it to the children, speedy, fast.

Rosie Stoddart (8)
Stratherrick Primary School, Inverness

The Witch's Brew

Into my cauldron I will put . . .
A big smelly sock and a dead sheep's foot

An old man's jeans and a big fat egg
Don't do it! They will all beg

Abracadabra, hocus pocus, dirty feet
Now add some juicy meat

One dead fly and a wild wasp's sting
The eye of a sheep and the blood of the king

Stolen rocks, a gold ring and a mouldy rock
For good flavour, a strawberry frock

Abracadabra, hocus pocus, dirty feet
Now add some juicy meat

Wing of bat and head of warlock
Tail of newt and dirty old sock

And don't forget the pint of king's blood
Mixed in with the scary trap of mud

Abracadabra, hocus pocus, dirty feet
Now it is ready to *eat!*

Joshua Glass (7)
Stratherrick Primary School, Inverness

Fear

Fear is dark and black,
Like melting tar smothered over a chipped stone pavement.

Fear feels as if you've been bitten by a jaguar's sharp teeth
And as if your heart is gone but loud beating is still heard
And as though one thousand dangerous creatures are watching you.

Fear reminds me of people waking up from endless nightmares,
Of disgusting werewolves and vampires in a dark, gloomy mansion.

Fear smells like sweat running off the face of a terrified child
And of a dead human rotting away in its coffin at midnight.

Fear looks like a gloomy, foggy and milky moonlight in a dark
forest of wolves
And foxes, bloodthirsty and hungry, with red eyes.

Fear sounds like a werewolf howling on a mucky rock with claws
like razors
And the sound of footsteps and lost souls moaning.

Fear tastes like bitter and slimy, sour bread,
It also tastes like swamp water, terror with slime and blood.

Adam Streets (10)
The Community School of Auchterarder (Primary), Auchterarder

Laughter

Laughter is multicoloured like a fast, cool car,
Painted with every colour in the world.
Laughter tastes like flying saucers filled with sugar in space.
Laughter feels excellent in your garden with friends and family
And at the beach too.
Laughter looks wild and cool, like somewhere exotic.
Laughter sounds like laughter high in the hills.
Laughter smells like sugar, sugar and more sugar.
Laughter reminds me of my holiday in England.

Aaron MacDonald (10)
The Community School of Auchterarder (Primary), Auchterarder

Darkness

Darkness is red like fire in the pitch-black midnight.
It feels as cold as the Arctic sea in winter.
It looks like the really scary Grim Reaper ready to slash.
It sounds like bats screaming in the death-black of a graveyard.
It smells like burning smoke from a crackling bonfire in the
centre of the woods.
It reminds me of a haunted graveyard on Hallowe'en.
It tastes like a red-hot chilli pepper burning through the throat.

Campbell Grant (10)
The Community School of Auchterarder (Primary), Auchterarder

Fear

Fear is as black as the glittering onyx lying in the jeweller's shop,
It reminds me of spiders running across the cold, damp floor,
It feels like a chain rotting and clinking nervously in the darkness.
Fear looks like a ghost in the corner, waiting to haunt someone.
Fear tastes like rotten onions that have been lying on the dresser
for three years,
It smells like old socks that haven't been washed,
It sounds like a guillotine being sharpened in the distance!

Madeleine Milburn (10)
The Community School of Auchterarder (Primary), Auchterarder

Darkness

Darkness is black like the black sky with stars.
It reminds me of the Godfather movie.
Darkness is like goths at night.
It tastes like human blood.
It feels like a bullet that has killed someone.
It sounds like a bullet being shot at someone.
It looks dark with ghosts.
It smells like a dead human rotting away!

Daniel Brown (9)
The Community School of Auchterarder (Primary), Auchterarder

Love

Love is red like a rose in a vase.
Love is red like the blood from a hound.
Love reminds me of a peaceful song.
Love sounds like an early morning lark, singing a sweet song.
Love feels like my heart thumping.
Love smells like cherry lipgloss from a girl's lips.
Love looks like a heart beating inside you.

Lachlan Rooney (10)
The Community School of Auchterarder (Primary), Auchterarder

Love

Love is pink,
It tastes like a sugary-tasting sweet.
It smells like newly-made candyfloss in the hot sun.
It sounds like two mermaids singing on a bridge.
It reminds me of seeing things go free.
It feels like very soft feathers.
It looks like a newly-flowered pink rose.

James Ross (9)
The Community School of Auchterarder (Primary), Auchterarder

Love

Love is pink like rose quartz in the jewellers,
It looks like a heart pumping blood round the body.
Love sounds like songbirds singing in the morning,
It smells like roses, pink in bloom.
Love reminds me of people French kissing on the TV,
It tastes like spaghetti Bolognese being eaten by two.
Love feels like fun and laughter put together.

Duncan McIntosh Wither (9)
The Community School of Auchterarder (Primary), Auchterarder

Happiness

Happiness is pink like a little girl's dress with a bow.
It feels like sticky sweets and a river of chocolate.
It looks like pillows, cold tropical juice and warm covers.
It tastes like fudge ice cream.
It sounds like people laughing and dropping stones into water.
It reminds me of sweets and chocolate.

Annabel Walker (10)
The Community School of Auchterarder (Primary), Auchterarder

Darkness

Darkness is black like a dark cave and a black coal fire.
Darkness is a black cold night at a funfair with people screaming.
It feels scary and dark.
It feels like I am scared and frightened.
It tastes like a Blackjack sizzling on my tongue.
It smells like black dark smoke coming out of a tall castle.

Hayley Clow (10)
The Community School of Auchterarder (Primary), Auchterarder

Anger

Anger is black like fighting and going mad,
It sounds like shouting and screaming,
It tastes like salt and vinegar crisps and pepper,
It feels like dying!
It reminds me of nuts, *yuck!*
It reminds me of liquorice,
It looks like a very old man!

Ewan Lambie (10)
The Community School of Auchterarder (Primary), Auchterarder

Happiness

Happiness is blue like the deep ocean.
Happiness is watching Rangers play football.
It reminds me of swimming in the ocean.
It tastes like bananas off a banana tree.
It feels like glory.
It looks like victory.
It smells like aftershave.

Ryan Carstairs (10)
The Community School of Auchterarder (Primary), Auchterarder

Young Writers Information

We hope you have enjoyed reading this book - and that you will continue to enjoy it in the coming years.

If you like reading and writing poetry drop us a line, or give us a call, and we'll send you a free information pack.

Alternatively if you would like to order further copies of this book or any of our other titles, then please give us a call or log onto our website at www.youngwriters.co.uk

Young Writers Information
Remus House
Coltsfoot Drive
Peterborough
PE2 9JX

(01733) 890066